SPRING

in the Forest

A *Seasons in the Forest* book

Field Guides for Little Naturalists

First Edition
ISBN 979-8-9864703-4-4

For Teresa and Tony,
who taught me about ever-changing nature.

Mother Heron has
very long legs

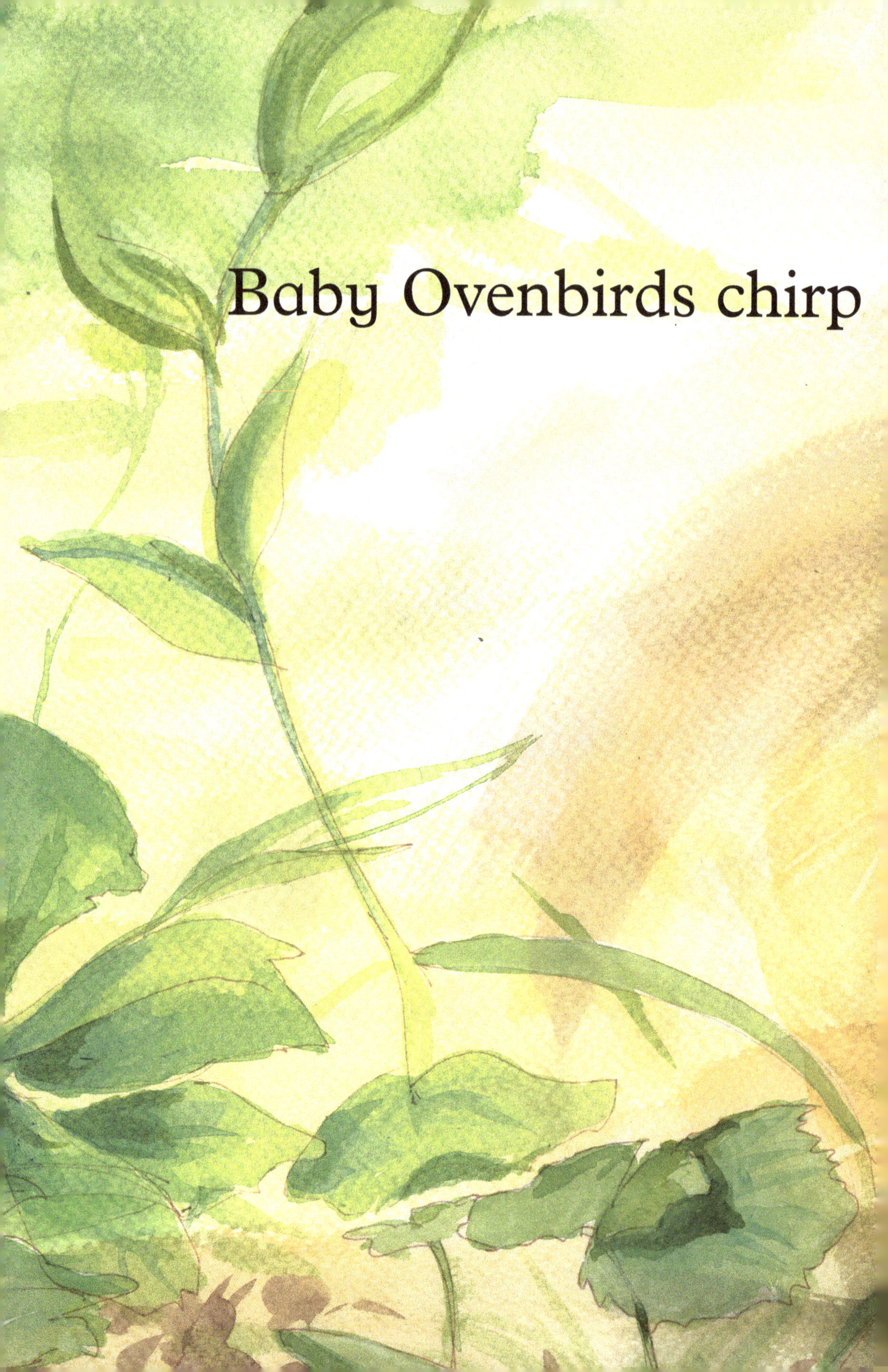

Baby Ovenbirds chirp

Salamander lays
slimy eggs

Sleepy Bullfrogs burp.

Rue Anemone waves,
"Look at me,
Look at me!"

Ladyslippers nod.

Trillium peeks from
behind a tree.

Mosses soften logs.

Melting ice
makes way
for greening.

Tiny fronds uncurl.

Dappled sunlight
chases winter.

Spring can
now unfurl.

Spring Peeper

Wood Frog

Eastern Red-backed Salamander

Eastern Newt

Ring-necked Snake

Painted Turtle

Snapping Turtle

Spring in the northern forest is a lively time. Bright sun warms the earth and flowers poke up through old leaves while new leaves are still in their buds. Many birds have returned and are now singing and building nests. Salamanders, frogs, toads, turtles and snakes have awakened from their long winter sleep.

The amphibians travel to forest pools to lay eggs during the night when it is raining. Eggs hatch and larvae and tadpoles slowly grow legs and lungs. Later on they will step out onto land and wander the forest floor.

About the author:

Christine Copeland lives in the forest of Massachusetts with her husband Bill, a pediatrician, naturalist and teacher, and their dogs and cat. Her sons have fledged but return seasonally. She is grateful to be visited by many birds and other animals throughout the year. Christine has a BFA from Cornell University and a Masters in Education from Antioch New England. She is an author/illustrator and also paints in oil. Her work can be seen at <u>christinecopelandbooks.com</u> and <u>bcc-studios.com/paintings</u>.

www.ingramcontent.com/pod-product-compliance
Lightning Source LLC
Chambersburg PA
CBHW042334030426
42335CB00027B/3341